> # George and Martha
> by James Marshall
> Houghton Mifflin; 1972

George and Martha contains five short stories about those hippo friends. Although it is not a single long story, reading about the same characters each day is a way of introducing children to longer books. Enjoy a full week of stories about the charming hippos' misadventures.

Think About Each Story:

''Split Pea Soup''
Why didn't George tell Martha that he hated split pea soup?
What did he do with the soup instead of eating it?
Was Martha angry when she found out? Why or why not?
What does this story teach us about being a good friend?

''The Flying Machine''
Why wouldn't the basket fly?
Why did it fly when George got out?
Can you think of a way George could have made the balloon fly with him in it?
Why was Martha glad he didn't fly away?

''The Tub''
What was George's bad habit?
Why do you think he peeked through other people's windows?
What happened when he peeked in Martha's bathroom window?
Do you think she was really angry at George? Did she stay mad?
What does this story teach us?

''The Mirror''
What did Martha do every chance she got?
How did George help break her of her habit?
Do you think it is bad to be thinking about how you look all of the time? Why or why not?
What does this story teach us about friendship?

''The Tooth''
How did George break his tooth?
What did Martha do to help him when he was feeling bad?
How did George solve his problem?
What did George say friends are for?

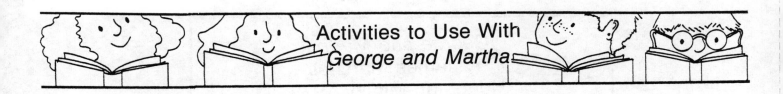
• Make George and Martha

Create pictures of George or Martha using the classified ads from the newspaper.

Give each child a large sheet of newspaper. Guide them through the following drawing steps to create their favorite hippo.

Children may use any of the following to add clothing to their hippos.

paint   construction paper

marking pens   wallpaper samples

cloth scraps   crayons

Create George and Martha puppets following these directions. Each child will need a copy of page 6.

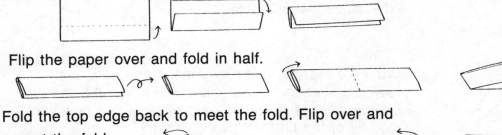

1. Make the basic fold using a 9'' X 18'' (22.8 X 45.7 cm) piece of gray construction paper. Fold in thirds lengthwise.

Flip the paper over and fold in half.

Fold the top edge back to meet the fold. Flip over and repeat the fold.

Fingers go in the open spaces.

2. They are to color, cut out, and paste the hippo pieces to their basic puppet fold.

Sharing Chapter Books

- **Pea Soup**

   Make pea soup in class. Collect the ingredients and equipment needed to make the soup. (It is fun as well as educational to take a field trip to a local market to buy the necessary ingredients.) Assign different jobs to groups of children. Cooking, eating, and clean-up each motivate oral and written activities.

   If you feel making soup is more than you want to attempt, buy several different brands of canned pea soup and make a comparison test. Compare looks, smell, and taste of the various types. Record the results on a chart or a graph.

- **Letters to George**

   Have your students write letters to George explaining how good pea soup really is. This is a good opportunity to practice descriptive language as well as the form for a friendly letter.

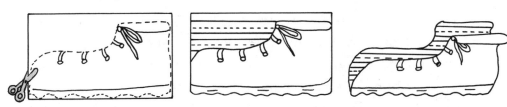

- **In My Shoe**

   George hid pea soup in his shoe. Create individual books about other things that could be hiding in a shoe.

   1. Draw a large shoe on a sheet of construction paper.

   Lay the shoe on a writing paper. Cut out two shoes at the same time. Staple or glue them together at the bottom.

   2. Draw a picture on the inside piece of paper.
      Make up a riddle about what is in the shoe. Write the riddle on the shoe.

   3. Pin the shoes to a bulletin board. Your students can read the riddles, guess what is in the shoe, then pull down the flap to see if they are correct.

• Fly Up High

Brainstorm to create a list of man-made things that can fly.

Design a flying machine for George. Draw a picture showing what the machine looks like. Put George in the picture also.

Write an adventure for George describing what might have happened if he had sailed off in his balloon.

Where would he go?

Would anyone go with him?

What would happen on his journey?

How would he get home?

• Bath Time

Martha was angry at George for looking in her window while she was taking a bath. She wanted her privacy. What could she have done to see that no one peeked in her bathroom window? What other things do we do when we might want our privacy?

Shower or tub? — Make a tally of how many people in class prefer to take a shower and how many prefer to bathe in a tub.

Visit your library. See if you can find any other stories about

George and Martha

bathtubs

good friends

• Mirror, mirror on the wall

Have your students take a good look into a real mirror, then draw pictures of themselves on ''mirror'' paper.

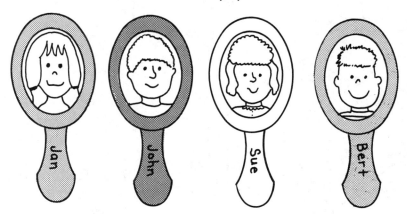

• The Tooth Fairy

Have a discussion about losing teeth. Ask questions such as:

Have you lost any of your teeth?
Did the tooth just fall out or did you lose it in an accident?
Have you ever had a tooth pulled by the dentist?
What happened to your tooth after you lost it?

Have your students pretend they are the tooth fairy. Have them think about what the job would involve. Then have them write stories. Here are some sample titles they might use.

A Night in the Life of the Tooth Fairy
What Do I Do With All of These Teeth?
Caught in the Act!

• Friendship

Use the stories of George and Martha to develop a discussion of friendship. Guide your students to answer questions such as...

What makes a good friend?
Can friends fight and still be friends?
How do you make a new friend?
How do you feel when a friend moves away?

Note: Use this page with the directions for the basic folded puppet shown on page 2.

Hippo Puppets

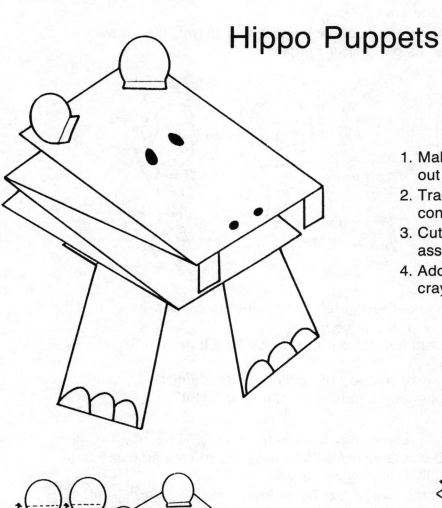

1. Make the basic folded puppet out of gray construction paper.
2. Trace the pattern pieces on construction paper.
3. Cut out the pieces and assemble as shown.
4. Add details with markers or crayons.

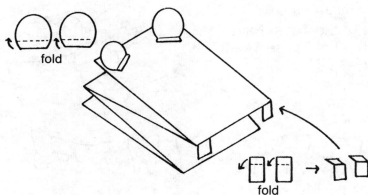

fold

fold

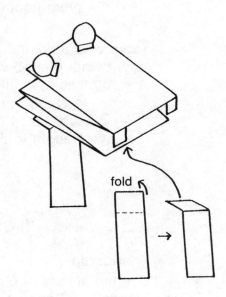

fold

hippo ear
cut 2
gray

hippo tooth
cut 2
white

hippo leg
cut 2
gray

Frog and Toad Together
by Arnold Lobel
Harper and Row; 1971

Frog and Toad Together is a series of short stories. Books such as this can be used as a beginning step toward reading longer stories to your students. This book contains five stories. Just enough for a full week of fun with those funny friends, Frog and Toad.

Think About Each Story:

"The List"

Why did Toad make a list?
What did he put on his list?
Why wouldn't Toad run after the list when the wind blew it away?
How did Frog help Toad?
Was the list a help or a problem to Toad? Why?

"The Garden"

How did Toad get seeds for his garden?
What did he do to make the seeds grow?
What did Frog say would make the seeds grow?
Why is patience necessary for a gardener?
Do you know what happens underground while you are waiting for the new little plant to show?

"Cookies"

How did Frog describe the cookies Toad had made?
Why did the friends decide to stop eating the cookies?
How did they try to keep themselves from eating the cookies?
What was Toad going to do when he got home?
What is "will power"?
Do you think Toad has will power?
Do you have will power? What makes you lose your will power?

"Dragons and Giants"

How did Frog and Toad try to find out if they were brave or not?
Do you think they were brave? Why or why not?
Can someone be brave about some things and not brave about others? Give some examples.

"The Dream"

What was Toad doing in his dream?
What happened to Frog every time Toad did something else?
Why did Toad become frightened?
Did the story have a happy ending? How?
Have you ever had a scary dream? Tell us about it.

- **Lists**

Brainstorm to come up with a class list of times when lists can be helpful. (For example: shopping, running errands, etc.)

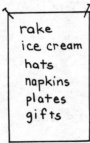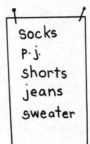

rake
ice cream
hats
napkins
plates
gifts

socks
p.j.
shorts
jeans
sweater

popcorn
pop
glasses
money
tickets

Make a list of what you would need to do for one of the following.

a birthday party
a visit to the dentist
a trip to another town
a soccer game

My List of Things to do Today:

Pretend you just woke up. Make a list of things you need to do today. When you are finished, cross out what you have already done. Will you be like Toad and only do what is on the list? Or will you change the list as the day goes by?

Today
1. Clean
2. Study
3. Party

 Sharing Chapter Books

• Gardens

Brainstorm to list plants that might be found in a...

vegetable garden   flower garden
orchard   vacant lot

Plant marigolds or nasturtiums in the classroom.
Keep a chart or notebook to record growth
information.

• Plant Experiments

You may want to do these simple experiments with the plants you
have grown in the classroom.

Plants Need Sunlight

1. Put two small green plants in a
   sunny window. Cover one plant
   with a paper bag.
2. Water each plant, but always
   keep the one plant under its
   bag.
3. Watch what happens over the
   next few weeks.

Plants Need Water

1. Put two small green plants in a
   sunny windows.
2. Water one plant when it is dry.
   DO NOT water the other plant.
3. Check every day to see what
   happens to the plants.

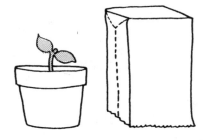

• Cookies

Brainstorm to list all kinds of cookies. Use the list to practice other skills.

Categorize the cookies by

> special ingredients (chocolate, peanut butter, etc.)
> shape (round, square, etc.)
> how made (cut, bar, drop)
> class favorites

Make the class' favorite cookie. This is a great opportunity to practice measurement, following written directions, and working in groups. This is not the time to practice "will power." Let everyone enjoy the fruits of their labor.

• Brave or Not?

Discuss how you can tell if a person is brave or not.

Ask questions such as...

> Have you (or someone you know) ever done something brave? What did you do? How did you feel?
> Can it be brave to walk away from a fight?
> Is someone always brave or always a coward?
> Is the strongest person always the bravest?

• Share a Dream

Discuss the different types of dreams people have.

Share a dream in one of the following ways:

> Tell your dream to the class.
> Draw a picture of an interesting dream.
> Write a story about your _____ dream.
> > funniest   scariest   most exciting

Note: Guide your students through these steps to create their own pop-up frog or toad.

Frog and Toad

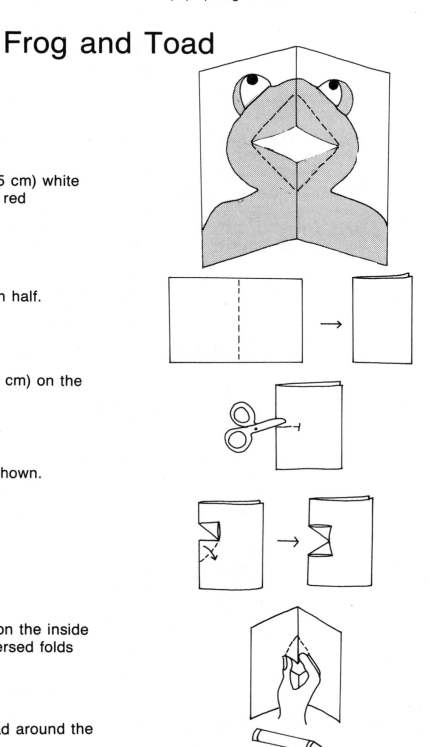

Materials

Construction paper:
9'' X 12'' (22.8 X 30.5 cm) white
2'' X 3'' (5 X 7.5 cm) red
crayons
colored paper scraps

1. Fold white paper in half.

2. Cut in about 2'' (5 cm) on the folded side.

3. Fold the flaps as shown.

4. Pull the flaps out on the inside and press the reversed folds shut.

5. Draw a frog or toad around the pop-up mouth.

You may wish to do one or more of the following:
Make cookies or seeds from scraps of paper. Put them in the toad's or frog's hands.
Make a curly red tongue. Paste it to the bottom of the mouth.
Paste the frog or toad into a cover made out of blue construction paper.

The Josefina Story Quilt
by Eleanor Coerr
Harper and Row; 1986

It was 1850 and Faith's family was preparing to travel to California in a covered wagon. Josefina, Faith's old pet hen, wasn't considered useful and only useful animals could go on the long journey. Father finally agreed that Josefina could go along, but only if she didn't cause any trouble. Well, she did cause trouble. But she also gave her life frightening off thieves. Throughout the story, Faith works on quilt patches chronicling the family's journey and adventures.

Questions about the story:

Where were Faith and her family going?

What could they take along?

Why do you think Father finally let Josefina go on the journey?

What trouble did Josefina get into?

In what ways did Josefina surprise everyone?

How did Faith feel when Josefina died?

What did she do?

What did Faith do to help remember events on the journey?

Think About It:

What did you learn about traveling by covered wagon while listening to this story? (Teacher — You may need to guide children by asking questions such as "How did they get food?" or "How did they get across rivers when there was no bridge?")

Faith used her story quilt to help her remember the journey. What other ways might she have chosen to help her remember the trip? What do we use today to help us remember important events in our lives?

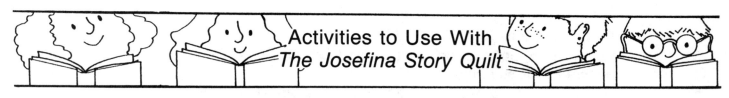
- **Traveling by Covered Wagon**

(These activities may be done as a class, by small groups, or by individual children.)

Tell where your covered wagon is traveling.

Describe what you would take in your wagon. Think about how important each item would be on the trip or when you reach your destination.

Decide where your journey will begin and end. Take a map of the U.S.A. and mark your route.

Write a description of one day of your journey.

- **Covered Wagons**

It is fun to make covered wagons. Here are three different methods you may use.

Reproduce the patterns on page 15. Children cut out the pieces and glue them to a sheet of thin cardboard. Other details may be added using scraps of paper.

Reproduce the directions on page 16. Children follow these directions to create a three-dimensional covered wagon from a milk carton, pipe cleaners, cloth, and cardboard.

Divide your class into groups of four. Challenge each group to come up with a way to make a model of a covered wagon. Each group must:

Decide what should be on each covered wagon.

Decide what materials they will need and who will be responsible for bringing each item.

Construct the wagon. Share the completed wagon with the class.

- **Plan "Share a Quilt" Day**

Let children, parents, or guests bring their special quilts to class to show to your students.

Encourage each participant to explain where their quilt came from and why it is special.

Take photographs of each quilt and speaker.

Have the class compose a paragraph about the quilt's story.

Put the photographs and stories into a class book.

- **Design a Quilt**

Discuss how quilts usually have some sort of a pattern. Provide children with a variety of opportunities to practice creating a design. For example...

Draw a pattern on graphing paper.

Use attribute blocks to create a pattern. When you have created a pattern you like, copy it on drawing paper.

Use tempera paint and objects to print a quilt pattern.

Design a nine-block quilt on paper. Have each square show a symbol. The symbols might represent:

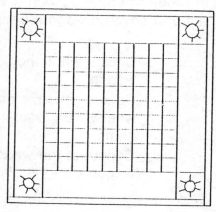

- a fairy tale
- a summer vacation
- a holiday such as Christmas
- a birthday party
- an event from history
- a special place such as Yosemite Park

Journey West

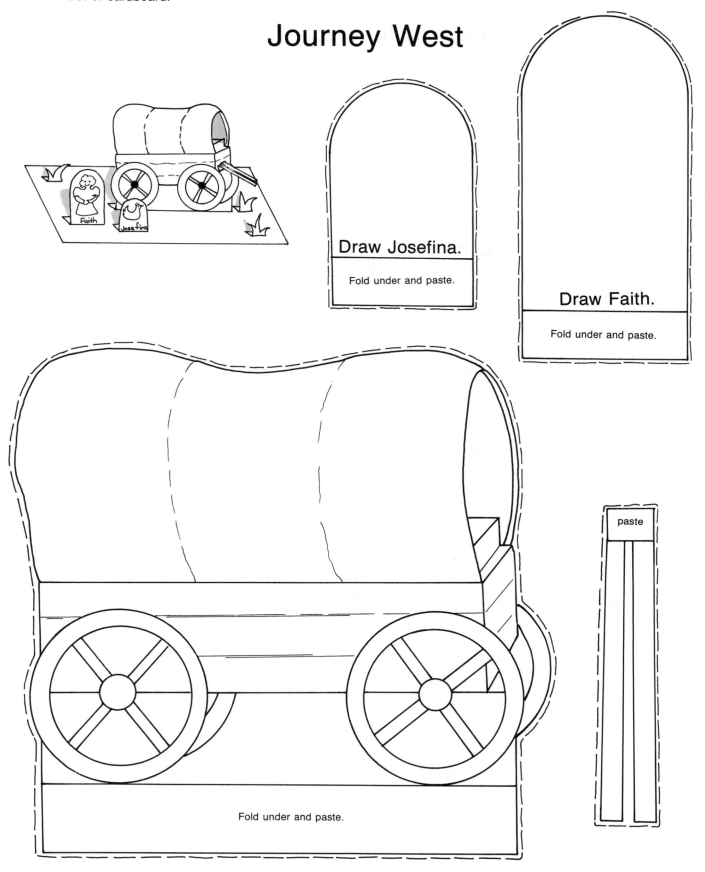

Draw Josefina.

Fold under and paste.

Draw Faith.

Fold under and paste.

paste

Fold under and paste.

Note: Here are steps for creating a simple covered wagon using a half-gallon milk carton, pipe cleaners, a scrap of cloth, and cardboard wheels.

Make a Covered Wagon

Materials:
1 milk carton
3 pipe cleaners
4 cardboard circles
4 paper fasteners
scrap of cotton fabric

Cut off one side of the milk carton.

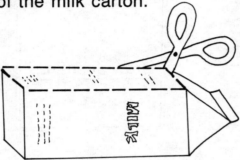

Bend three long pipe cleaners and attach them to the carton with glue or tape.

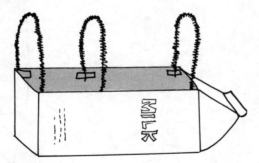

Glue the cloth scrap over the pipe cleaners.

Add the cardboard wheels

with brass paper fasteners.

         Sharing Chapter Books

Commander Toad in Space
by Jane Yolen
Coward-McCann, Inc.; 1980

Commander Toad and the crew of Star Warts have an exciting adventure on a mysterious water planet deep in outer space. It takes great ingenuity and courage for the crew to escape from the clutches of the terrible Deep Wader.

Commander Toad in Space is not written in chapters, but it does contain several natural breaks. For example:

page 7 to page 27
page 28 to page 43
page 44 to page 64

Questions about the story:

Name the members of the crew and describe their various jobs.

What was the mission of the Star Warts?

Why couldn't they land on the new planet with their sky skimmer?

How did they solve the problem of landing on the water planet?

Describe Deep Wader.

How did the crew try to escape from Deep Wader? What did not work?

How did Commander Toad fix the lily pad raft?

Think About It:

What did the Commander say to Lt. Lily when she asked about being brave? Do you agree with his answer? Why?

If you could trade places with someone on the Star Warts for a day, which crew member would you choose to be? Why?

Can you think of any stories you have heard or seen that are like parts of this story?

What kind of landing vehicle could be used on a desert planet, a fiery planet, or a gas planet?

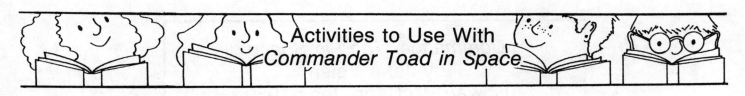
- **The Star Warts Crew**

  The members of the Star Warts crew need special equipment and clothing for their adventures. Give each student a copy of the toad on page 20. Have them create the astronaut clothing and gear needed by their favorite crew member.

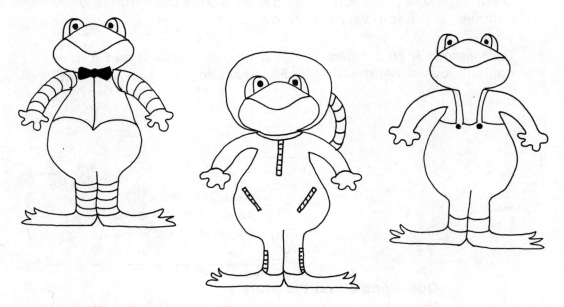

- **The (name of the ship)**

  Divide the class into groups of four students. Challenge each group to design a space ship and an unusual crew. Each group would be responsible for doing the following...

1 Make a drawing, painting, or 3-D version of their ship and its crew.

2 Name the ship and each crew member. Decide what each crew member does on board the ship.

> Captain Hook is the leader. He gives orders.

3 Write a brief space adventure for the crew.

4 Share the completed project with the class.

• **Space Trek**

Create an interesting new world on a large bulletin board. Make the planet from a large sheet of butcher paper.

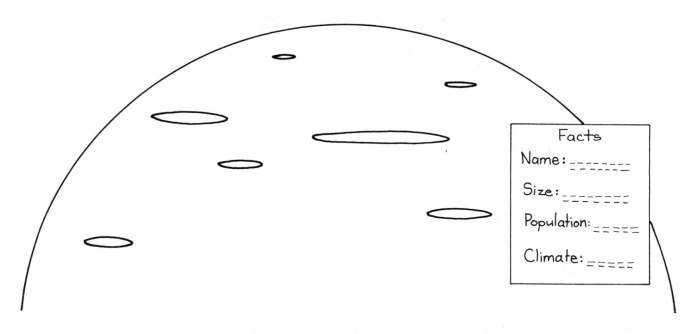

Facts
Name: _____
Size: _____
Population: _____
Climate: _____

Have your students develop a list of "facts" about the planet. (For example: What is it made of? Is there any atmosphere? What type of plants and animals would live there? Etc.) Write these facts on a chart to go with the bulletin board.

Add one or more of the following to your bulletin board:

Place the Star Warts crew on the planet.

Draw or paint creatures and plants that might live on the planet.

Place one or more of the ships created by your students on or circling the planet.

Tell or write about an adventure that might happen with one or more of the creatures or plants found on the planet.

Note: Reproduce this page on construction paper. Have each student draw appropriate clothing and gear for his/her favorite member of the Star Warts crew.

Toad in Space

Sharing Chapter Books

My Father's Dragon
by Ruth Stiles Gannett
Random House; 1948

Elmer Elevator befriends a talking cat and learns of a young dragon being kept prisoner by the lazy animals of Wild Island. The poor dragon is kept on a rope and made to fly the animals back and forth across the crocodile infested river. Elmer runs away to Wild Island determined to rescue the dragon. He cleverly uses the items in his knapsack to escape from each of the wild animals, finally reaching his goal.

Questions about the story:

How would you describe the baby dragon?

How did Elmer know what to take on his journey?

Why didn't the cat go with Elmer?

How did Elmer get to Tangeria?

Why did the wild boars think Wild Island was being invaded?

How did Elmer use the_____ to escape from danger?

empty grain bag	magnifying glasses
chewing gum	lollipops
brush, comb, & ribbons	jackknife

Think About It:

What do you think was happening at Elmer's home while he was off on his adventure?

What do you think happened to the dragon after Elmer rescued him?

The book describes the dragon as "about the size of a black bear." How big would that make the dragon? Where can you find out that information?

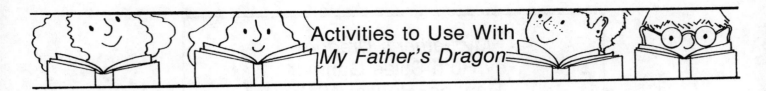

- **Using Illustrations**

  The illustrations in a story can be used to give additional information about the story. They can also be used to stimulate creative expression. For example:

  Use the map at the beginning of chapter two to see what your students can infer from the illustrations and topography.

  Make a copy of Wild Island on a large chart. Have your students add the physical features and the animals.

  Select illustrations such as those on pages 28, 29, and 84 to stimulate creation of oral or written original stories.

- **Make a Mural**

  Brainstorm to list the most important events in the story. Divide the class into small groups. Have each group paint a mural of that scene from the story. Display the murals around the classroom in the sequence the events occur in the story.

- **Listen and Draw**

  The book contains an artist's idea of how the little dragon looked. Read the description of the dragon at the top of page 18 and have your students draw or paint the little dragon as they imagine he would look.

- **A Flying Dragon**

  Have your students write stories explaining how they would have rescued the dragon. Display the stories on a "flying dragon" bulletin board. This is simple to create. Just follow the steps below.

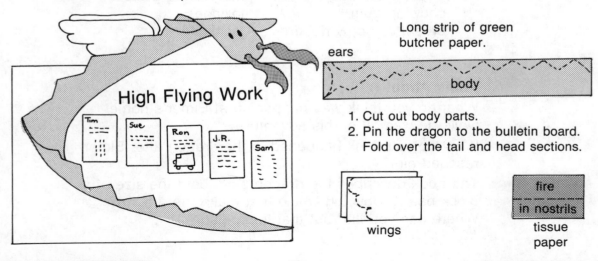

Long strip of green butcher paper.

ears

body

1. Cut out body parts.
2. Pin the dragon to the bulletin board. Fold over the tail and head sections.

wings

fire
in nostrils
tissue paper

High Flying Work

The Secret Moose
by Jean Rogers
Greenwillow Books; 1985

Life in Alaska could be very exciting. One day, following tracks behind his house, Gerald found an injured moose. He keeps his discovery a secret from his family and sets out to learn about moose. He figures out how to feed the moose when she can no longer reach food on her own. The last time Gerald sees his moose, he has a big surprise. The moose is standing with her newborn calf. The next day both the mother and her baby are gone. Only their tracks are left, leading back into the woods. Gerald covers up the tracks to try and insure the moose's safety.

Questions about the story:

Where did Gerald and his family live?

When did Gerald first see the moose?

How did Gerald find the moose?

Describe the moose's injuries.

Why was Gerald careful about getting too close to the moose?

How did Gerald know the moose was female?

How did he help the moose?

Think About It:

Do you think the moose will ever return to Gerald's area? Why or why not?

What should you do if you find an injured wild animal?

What kinds of dangers do wild animals face when the wander into areas where people live?

Can you name other animals that live in the far north?

- **Map Skills**

  Have your students study a map of Alaska. See if they can locate where Gerald lived. (You may want to give each child a copy of the map on page 26. Have them mark where the adventure of Gerald and his moose took place.)

  Think about how the area is described in the story. Can you find other places on the map that show where a moose might live?

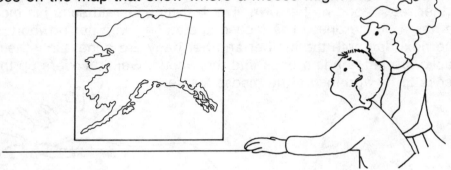

- **Beginning Report Writing**

  Discuss what the children have learned about moose from hearing this story.

  Take your class to the library and locate other sources of information about moose. Decide which parts are appropriate for your grade level. Read these parts aloud to your students.

  Guide the class in writing a short group report on moose. Older students may be ready to write individual paragraphs with the information they have heard you read.

- **What Happened Next?**

  Discuss what might happen to the moose and her calf after they left Gerald's property. Have children work in pairs or individually to write their version of what might happen.

- **Moose, Mooses, Meese?**

Have the children help you create a list of animals. Write the names on the chalkboard. Have the children see if they can give you the plural form. For example:

cat —cats   mouse — mice
horse — horses   goose — geese
deer — deer   moose — moose

- **Eat a Moose?**

Explain to your students that in parts of the world people do hunt and eat moose meat in the same ways we eat cattle. However, if they go into a restaurant and order moose, they will probably be served "mousse." The words sound alike, but the taste would be very different.

Brainstorm to make a list of homophones. Discuss what each word in the pair means. You may need to provide a "starter" list such as:

moose — mousse   herd — heard
blue — blew   steal — steel
stare — stair   doe — dough

Assign one pair of words to each student to illustrate.

Make mousse with your class. Serve it as a snack as you reread parts of *The Secret Moose.* You can use your favorite mousse recipe or use packaged instant mousse mix. Either way your students will have an opportunity to practice measurement skills and reading to follow directions.

- **Moose Shape Book**

Follow the directions on page 27. Use this as the cover for...

the class' moose report
the original stories written by your students
a book of illustrated homophones
a book of singular and plural forms

Note: Reproduce the map of Alaska to use with the activity on page 24.

Alaska

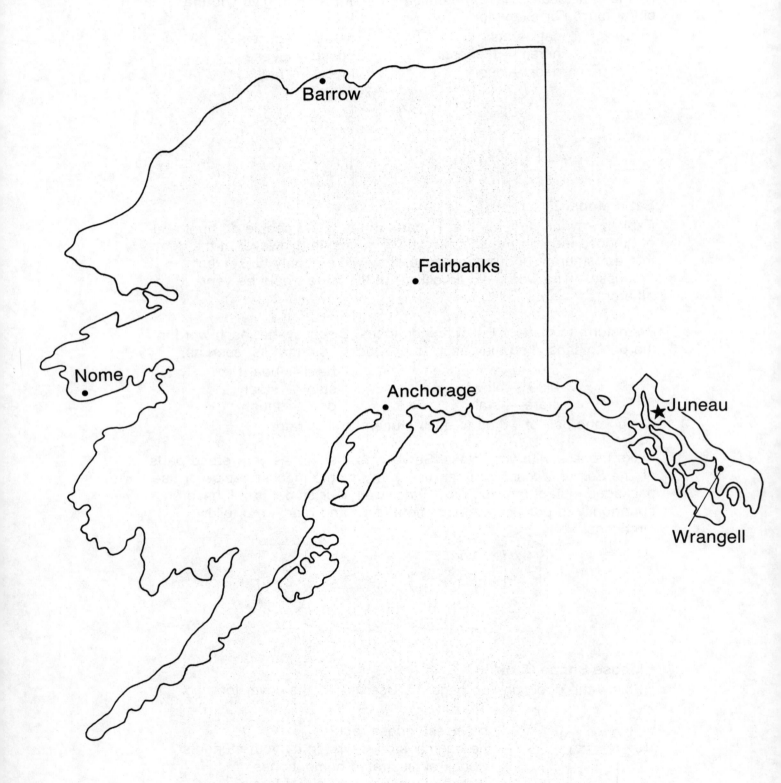

Note: Cut writing paper into 6'' X 12'' (15 X 30.5 cm) sheets to fit this cover. Children will need to leave a one inch margin at the top of each sheet.

A Moose Shape Book

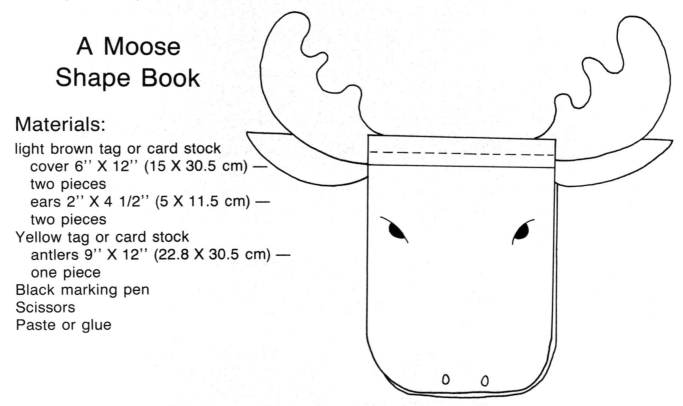

Materials:

light brown tag or card stock
    cover 6'' X 12'' (15 X 30.5 cm) —
    two pieces
    ears 2'' X 4 1/2'' (5 X 11.5 cm) —
    two pieces
Yellow tag or card stock
    antlers 9'' X 12'' (22.8 X 30.5 cm) —
    one piece
Black marking pen
Scissors
Paste or glue

Steps to Follow:

1. Make a hinged cover.

   Cut a one-inch (2.5 cm) strip from the top of one piece of the brown tag.

   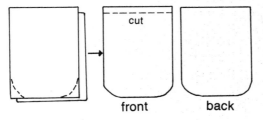

2. Staple the stories to the back cover. Tape the two pieces back together, leaving a small space in between.

   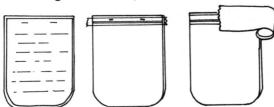

   Place the front cover on top of the stories. Staple the covers together. Cover staples with tape.

3. Make the moose.

   Draw the face with black marking pen. Add eyes and nostrils.

   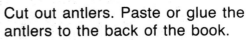

   Cut out antlers. Paste or glue the antlers to the back of the book.

   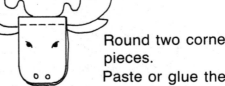

   Round two corners on the ear pieces.
   Paste or glue the ears behind the antlers.

4. Add the title with black marking pen.

Adam is having problems in school. The class bully makes fun of him because he is fat and has trouble reading. Then he meets a little dragon who is running away from Dragonland because he hates school. With the help of his new friend, Adam learns how to handle a bully and to have the confidence to do the things he has failed at before.

Questions about the story:

Why did Adam hate school?

Why did Little Dragon run away from Dragonland?

How did Adam feed chocolate to the little dragon?

What happened when Adam climbed the tree? How did he get down?

What finally happened to the little dragon?

Think About It:

How did teaching the little dragon to read, write, turn somersaults, etc. help Adam?

Why couldn't anyone except Adam see the dragon?

What parts of this story could/could not happen in real life?

Why do you think Larry Hall was so mean to Adam?

What can you do to make a bully stop bothering you or someone else?

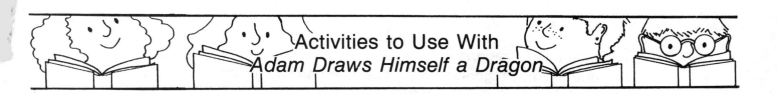

- **Teach a Friend**

  Adam taught the dragon to do many things. Challenge your students to teach something they do well to a classmate who cannot do it.
  For example:

  how to say something in another language
  how to play a game
  how to make something (kite, cookies, model car, etc.)
  how to read a map
  how to sew on a button
  how to fix a broken toy

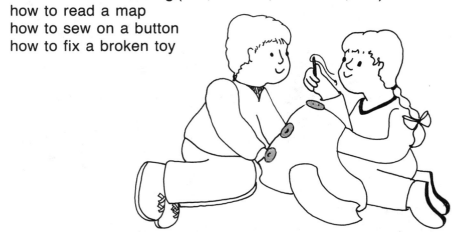

- **Action Words**

  This story is full of interesting verbs. Have children listen for the action words as you reread a section of the story. For example, the last two paragraphs on page 41 and the first paragraph on page 42 contain the following words.

climbed	braced	poking
grabbed	watched	groaned
panted	grumbled	reached

Brainstorm to add to the list. Do one or more of the following activities.

Have your students act out each of the actions on the list.

Make an alphabet book of actions. They may draw their own illustrations or find appropriate pictures in magazines.

Write and illustrate sentences using words from the list.

Challenge older students to write a paragraph (that makes sense) containing as many of the action words as possible.

• Three-Headed Dragons

The dragons in Dragonland were described as having three heads with each head blowing out a different color of fire.

Draw three-headed dragons.

Give each child three strips of tissue paper (red, yellow, and blue) for the dragon's fire.

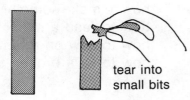

tear into
small bits

Put the tissue in place and brush with liquid starch.

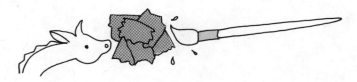

• Dragon Songs

Adam made up little songs for the dragon. Make up a dragon song or poem about a friendly or a fierce dragon. (Do this as a class activity if your students are just learning to write.) You may want to provide a beginning phrase. For example...

My little dragon loves _____.

My little dragon loves to bake.
He makes yummy chocolate cake.
Chocolate cake is good to eat.
He holds the pieces in his feet.

My little dragon loves to fly.
His wings take him way up high.
When he's tired of flying around
He comes back down to the ground.

Write the words to the song or poem on a sheet of paper. Attach the paper to a sheet of drawing paper. Draw a picture to illustrate the song or poem.

A Toad for Tuesday
by Russell E. Erickson
Lothrop, Lee and Shepard Co.; 1974

Warton and his brother Morton are very different toads. Morton likes to stay close to home while Warton is always eager to be out doing something. In the middle of winter Warton decides to set off on a visit to old Aunt Toolia, ignoring Morton's warnings about the dangers that could occur. Everything goes well for awhile. Then Warton is captured by a hungry owl. As Warton attempts to escape an unusual friendship develops.

A Toad for Tuesday is not written in chapters, but it does have several natural breaks. For example:

page 9 to the middle of page 31
mid-page 31 to the middle of page 46
mid-page 46 to page 63

Questions about the story:

Where did Warton plan to go? Why?

What was Morton's warning to his brother?

How did Warton plan to keep warm?

When Warton rescued the mouse he received another warning. What did the mouse say?

Why did the mouse give Warton a red scarf?

How did Warton get hurt?

What was Owl's plan for Warton?

Describe what Warton did in Owl's home.

How did Warton try to escape? What happened?

Why did Warton rescue the owl from the fox?

Think About It:

Describe Warton and Morton. How were they alike?

How were they different? Why do you suppose one was eager for adventure and the other one wanted to stay at home?

How do you think the friendship developed between Warton and Owl?

What does this story teach us about friendship?

Do you think you are more like Warton or more like Morton? Why do you think so?

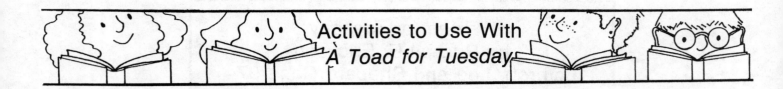
- **Morton's Famous Beetle Brittle**

  Create a recipe for this delicacy.
  Use the worksheet on page 34.
  List the ingredients and give step-by-step
  directions.

- **Pencil Sketches**

  Make pencil sketches of Warton or Owl.
  Write a descriptive paragraph to go with the picture.

- **Home Sweet Home**

  Make a diorama of Owl's home. (This is a great
  co-operative learning activity.)

  Take a box (oatmeal, shoe box, etc.) with one open
  side. (You will need to cut an opening in the side if
  you use an oatmeal box.)

  Paint the inside of the box to look like walls and a
  floor.

  Make furniture from construction paper, little boxes,
  pictures from magazines, cardboard, etc.

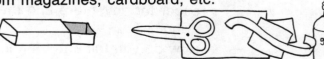

  Add an owl and a toad made from paper or clay.

- **Friendship**

  Create a class book on friendship. This book could be on a theme such as:

  > How to Be a Good Friend
  > Poems About Friendship
  > My Best Friend
  > Unexpected Friends
  > A Friend is...
  > It Isn't Always Easy to Be a Friend

  When the stories or poems have been written and illustrated, bind them into a simple tag or cardboard cover and place the book where children can read it in their free time.

- **Act it Out**

  Make stick puppets following the steps below. Have children work in pairs (or small groups) to create dialogue for one event from the story.

  > Select the event you want to act out.
  > Draw the characters on tag or thin cardboard.
  > Color the characters with crayons or marking pens.

  Cut them out and tape or paste to tongue depressors.

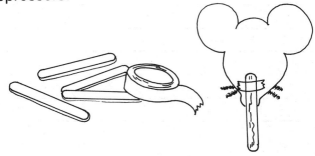

  Decide what each character is going to say. Share your play with the rest of the class.

 # Beetle Brittle

Ingredients:

Steps to Follow:

The Mouse and the Motorcycle
by Beverly Cleary
William Morrow & Company; 1965

Ralph is a small mouse who lives with his family in an old inn. An unexpected friendship develops between Ralph and Keith, a young boy on vacation at the Mountain View Inn. Ralph has many exciting adventures riding on Keith's mouse-sized toy motorcycle.

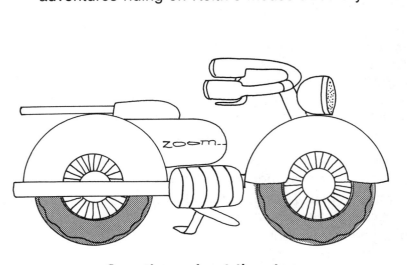

Questions about the story:

How did Ralph and Keith first meet?
What made the motorcycle run?
What were some of the dangers Ralph had to be careful of in the old inn?
How did Ralph escape from the vacuum cleaner?
How did Ralph lose the motorcycle?
How did Keith help the mice?
What did Ralph do to help when Keith was sick?
How did Ralph end up outside the hotel?
Why did Keith give Ralph the motorcycle?

Think About It:

Some things that happen in this story could really happen. Other things are make believe. Describe an event that is fantasy. Tell about an event that could be real.
What words could you use to describe Ralph?
What would you do if you found a mouse in your bedroom?

       Sharing Chapter Books

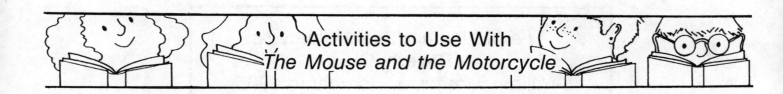
• **Ralph in Action**

Many times the illustrations in a book can tell you a lot about what is happening in the story.

> Decide which part of the story you enjoyed the most. Make an illustration that "tells" what happened.

> Show your picture to someone else in class. Does your picture clearly show what you wanted it to tell? Did the person recognize which part of the story you were illustrating? Do you need to change the picture in any way to make it clearer?

• **The Further Adventures of Ralph**

Have children write their own mouse adventures.

Students who have difficulty getting started may need to create a little outline for guidance. For example...

> Who is your story about?
> Where does the story take place?
> When does the story happen?
> What is the problem?
> How is the problem solved?

• **Make a Mouse**

Use the directions and pattern pieces on page 38 to create a three-dimensional mouse. Tuck one of the following into the paper tube.

> facts about mice
>
> what your mouse can do
>
> words that describe mice
>
> a mouse poem

• **Make a motorcycle**

Reproduce the pattern on page 37.

Children color, cut, and paste the pieces together to create a motorcycle for Ralph. Children may want to use this drawing to illustrate a scene from their original mouse stories.

Note: Reproduce this page. Children color, cut, and paste the pieces together on a sheet of construction paper to create a motorcycle. Let them add Ralph to the picture. Encourage them to create a background that "tells" a story.

Make a Motorcycle

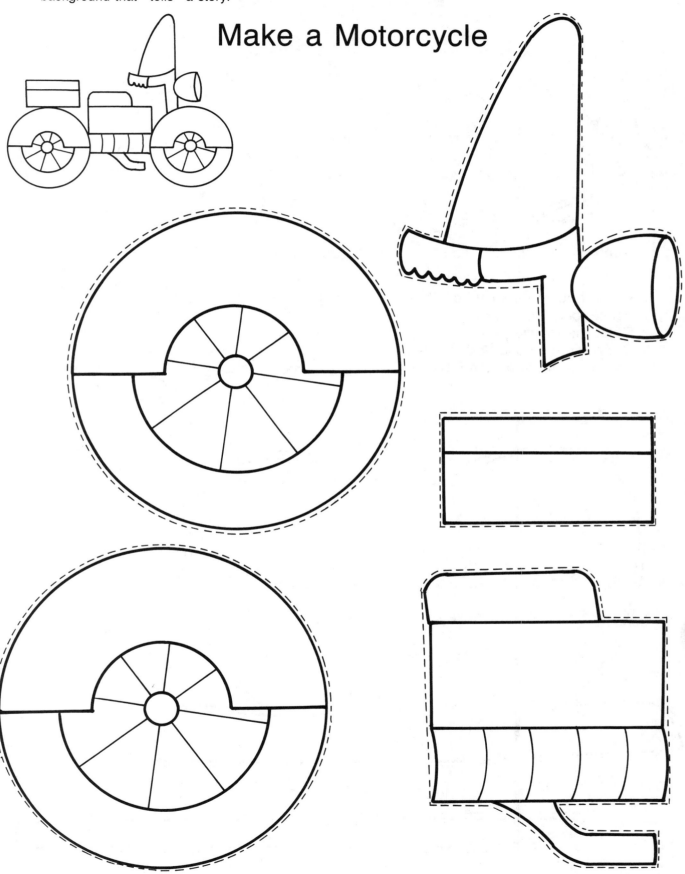

Make a Mouse

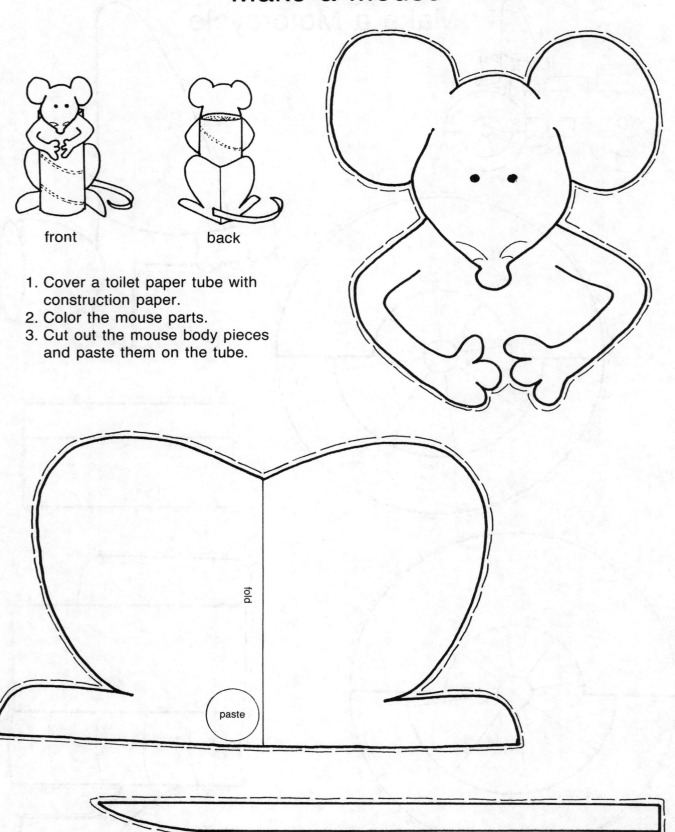

front   back

1. Cover a toilet paper tube with construction paper.
2. Color the mouse parts.
3. Cut out the mouse body pieces and paste them on the tube.

fold

paste

Curl the tail on a pencil.

> *How to Eat Fried Worms*
> by Thomas Rockwell
> Dell Publishing Company; 1973

Billy makes a bet that he can eat fifteen worms in fifteen days. He has also agreed that Alan gets to choose the worms. His opponent makes sure the worms are long and juicy! With the help of a wide range of condiments, Billy manages to swallow the worms. Even though Alan resorts to some trickery, Billy wins his fifty dollars. He also discovers that he has developed a taste for worms.

Questions about the story:

How did the bet between Billy and Alan happen?

Where was Alan going to get fifty dollars to bet with?

What did Billy have to do to win the money?

What were some of the ways Billy fixed the worms in order to eat them?

What did Billy's parents do when they found out he was eating worms? Why didn't they make him stop?

What did Alan start to do when it looked like Billy was going to win the bet?

What were some of the ways he tried to keep Billy from eating his daily worm?

What happened to Alan when he lost the bet?

What discovery did Billy make after eating worms for fifteen days in a row?

Think About It:

What effect did this bet have on the friendship between Alan and Billy? Why do you think Alan felt he needed to cheat to make Billy lose? Are there any type of bets that are safe for friends to make with one another?

Would you be willing to eat something like worms in order to win a big bet? What would your parents do if they found out?

What is the most unusual thing you have ever eaten? How did you happen to eat it?

What do you use to change the flavor of a food you have to eat but don't like? Does it help?

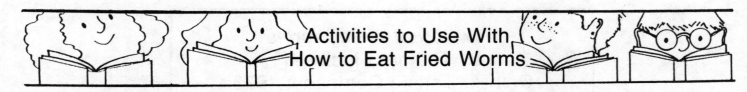

- **Snails, Eels, and Frog's Legs**

Brainstorm to list unusual foods. Discuss where the food is eaten. Have children decide which foods they think they would eat.

Tally how many children have ever tasted foods such as snails, eel, snake, frog's legs, kidneys, squid, etc. Graph the information you gather. (If your class has never been exposed to any of these types of foods, you may want to graph what they think they would be willing to try.)

Tasting Time — If you have a brave crew, provide some of the more exotic foods for a tasting day. This is for volunteers only of course!

- **Worm Recipes**

What do you think a worm would taste like? Write a description of the taste of raw or cooked worm.

Create a tasty way to prepare those yummy earthworms. (You may want to use the form on page 42.)

    Decide if the worm is going to be a snack, main course, soup, sandwich, dessert, etc.

    Plan your list of ingredients. How much of each ingredient will you need?

    Make a list of directions on how to fix your "wormy" delight.

Make an illustration to go with your recipe.

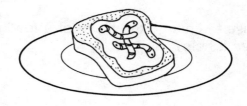

- **Pet Earthworms**

Earthworms are easy animals to keep in a classroom.

Gather them by digging in the ground or at night when they come to the surface. Put the earthworms in a large mouthed glass jar or a small aquarium. (You will only need six in a jar or a dozen or so in the aquarium.)

Fill the container half or two-thirds full of soil. Add some leaves from the ground where you found the worms. Place a layer of the leaves on top of the soil in your container.

Place the container in the coolest part of your classroom. Keep the container out of direct sunlight and away from sources of heat. Wrap the container in black construction paper. Remove the paper when you wish to observe the worms.

Sprinkle a few drops of water on the soil every few days. It needs to be moist but not too wet.

Use green leafy vegetables such as celery leaves or lettuce for food. You may also use cut-up vegetable scraps. Don't over feed the worms. Remove old food before it spoils.

Make the following observations:

How do the worms move around the container?

How so their mouths work as they eat?

Hold one gently and observe its body parts and how it feels.

Record your observations. Keep these observations on a chart or in a notebook. Add illustrations of the worms to show the body parts.

Only keep the earthworms while you are studying them. Be sure to return them to the area they were found when you are finished with them.

Note: Reproduce this form for your students to use as they create their own taste treats.

Worm ______________________

How to catch your worm:

Other ingredients:

Cooking directions:

Little House in the Big Woods
Laura Ingalls Wilder
Harper & Row; 1932/1959

Little House in the Big Woods is the first in Laura Ingalls Wilder's series about growing up in frontier times. In this volume, Laura and her family live in a snug log cabin in the woods of Wisconsin. Pa hunts, farms, tells wonderful stories, and plays his fiddle. Ma cooks, sews, and teaches her daughters the skills they need. The story helps modern children understand the hard work, the dangers, and the kinds of fun that made up pioneer life in the 1860's.

Questions about the story:

Can you describe the place where Laura and her family lived?

How did Ma and Pa get food and clothing for the family?

Can you explain how _____ was/were made?

     butter   bullets for hunting   new hats

What were some of the ways food was prepared for the winter?

How did the aunts, uncles, and grandparents help each other?

Why was it important to have a good watch dog in pioneer days?

Why was it important for children to obey their parents quickly?

Think About It:

Describe some ways in which life was different for little Laura and her family than it would be now.

Describe ways in which life was the same then as now.

Laura was five years old the first time she went to town. She was surprised at the size and contents of the store. Can you remember the first time you went to a large store? If so, describe how you felt and what you remember seeing.

What do you think you would miss the most if you suddenly were transported back to Laura's time?

Suppose you could choose to live in the big woods of Wisconsin in 1860. Would you go? Would you go to stay if your whole family could go too? Give some reasons for your answers.

 Sharing Chapter Books

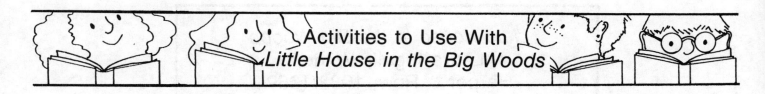
- **Long, Long Ago**

Invite older people into class to tell stories about when they were young. It is especially nice if they can tell about what happened when they were the same age as your students.

You can use these visits to practice various skills. For example:

> Have students retell what they remember of the story. (This can be done orally or in written form.)

> Find the location of the story on a map. If a journey occurred in the story, trace its path on the map.

> Keep a class journal of visitors. Include information about the speaker and a photo or drawing.

> Write thank-you notes to the speakers.

> Play a game, sing a song, or make something that was talked about by the visitor.

- **Then and Now**

Review how life was different and the same in Laura's time and today. Divide your class into two groups. Have one group bring something from home that Laura would have had. Have the other group bring something that Laura would not have had. (These may be pictures rather than actual objects.)

Give each child a large sheet of drawing paper. Have them fold the paper in half. Draw a scene from life in Laura's day on one half of the paper. Draw a scene from life today on the other half of the paper. Older students may also write descriptive paragraphs to accompany their pictures.

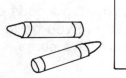

• Bread and Butter

Ma, Pa, and the girls had to make everything they ate. Provide your students with the opportunity to make their own bread and butter. You may want to serve honey out of the comb or maple syrup for sweetener.

Bread — Follow any bread recipe in your favorite cookbook. If you feel bread is too ambitious for your class, make biscuits or cornbread. They still get the feeling of creating their own food from scratch.

Butter — It is fun to see a real churn if you can borrow one. However, you can make successful butter using a glass jar with a tight lid. Fill the jar about two-thirds full with cream. Let each child in class have a turn shaking the jar. Twenty or thirty shakes each should be enough. Stop when the butter forms a lump in the jar. Rinse the butter with cool water until all of the milky liquid is gone. Serve the butter on the bread, biscuits, or cornbread the children made.

• Life in the Future

Little House in the Big Woods contains many descriptions of everyday life in the 1860's. Pretend it is the year 2060 and you are an older person trying to explain what life was like in the 1990's. Write a story describing one of these activities.

shopping for food or clothing
cooking a meal
a day at school
a game or activity you do for fun
father's or mother's work
a visit to a doctor or dentist
traveling to a new place
television or video games

Make an illustration to go with your story.

The Chocolate Touch
by Patrick Skene Catling
William Morrow and Co.; 1979

John Midas' greedy love of candy leads to a strange affliction. When he first discovers he has the "chocolate touch," John is thrilled. Chocolate is his favorite candy in the whole world. Soon he begins to experience doubt as everything his lips touch turns to chocolate. When he kisses his mother and she turns to chocolate, John finally expresses an unselfish emotion. This leads to a cure and everything (including mother) returns to its original state.

Questions about the story:

What was John's biggest fault?

What did the doctor tell John to do?

Where did the strange coin come from? What was it good for?

How did John get the chocolate touch?

Give some examples of what happened to John after he was stricken with the chocolate touch.

Why did he have so much difficulty convincing people of his problem?

What made John begin to think of someone besides himself?

How was John cured of his strange disease?

Think About It:

Why do you think John loved candy so much? Is there anything you love to eat as much as John loved candy?

What might have happened to John if he was not cured of the chocolate touch?

Why do you suppose John didn't turn himself into chocolate?

How is this story like *King Midas and the Golden Touch?* How is it different?

 Sharing Chapter Books

- **The** _____ **Touch**

  Create a new kind of "touch." Tell how you got this strange "touch."
  What happened when you touched things? How were you cured? (This
  can be done orally or as a written assignment.)

- **Candy**

  Brainstorm to list all types of candy. Use the list to create categories
  and to practice graphing skills.

Categories

Group by form (bars, drops, sticks...)
Group by main ingredient (chocolate, peanut butter,
peppermint...)
Group by how sold (individual, bag, box...)
Group by price
Group by class favorites

Graphing

Make a tally showing how many children have
tasted each type on the list. Use the information
collected to create a graph of class favorites.

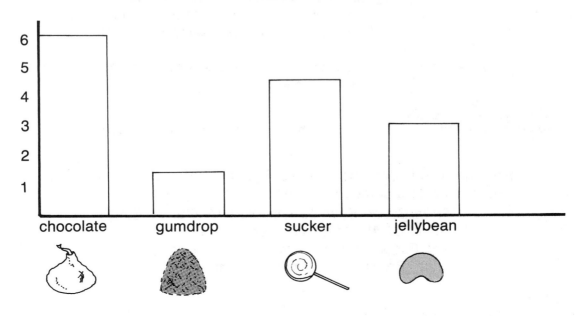

• The Chocolate Touch

It is fun to imagine what the world would look like if everything were changed into chocolate.

Have your students draw themselves, an animal or an object.

Place the drawing on top of a sheet of brown construction paper. Cut out the picture cutting through both pieces of paper at the same time. Place the chocolate version on top and glue or staple the two pieces together. By lifting the flap, they see the chocolate and non-chocolate versions of the same thing.

A chocolate mural can also be fun. Paint pictures of something or someone John might have touched. Use all shades of brown to represent different types of chocolate. You may want your students to paint directly onto the mural or have them each make separate paintings. When the paintings are dry, cut them out and paste them to the mural background. Add a picture of a perplexed John to complete the mural.

• Compare and Contrast

Have a chocolate tasting day. Have children taste small bits of milk chocolate, dark chocolate, semi-sweet, and unsweetened chocolate powder.

Make lists of words that describe each type (taste, smell, texture, etc.).

Discuss how each type might be used.

Here are two interesting sources if your children are interested in where chocolate comes from and how it is processed.

From Cacao Bean to Chocolate (A Start to Finish Book) by Ali Mitgutsch; Carolrhoda, 1971.
The Scoop on Ice Cream (Chapter 4) by Vicki Cobb; Little, Brown and Company, 1985.